Life Lessons from the School Bus

Anthony C. Baker

Parson's Porch & Company

Parson's Porch Books

Life Lessons from the School Bus

ISBN: Softcover 978-0692336250

Copyright © 2014 by Anthony C. Baker

All rights reserved. No part of this book may be reproduced or transmitted in any form or by any means, electronic or mechanical, including photocopying, recording, or by any information storage and retrieval system, without permission in writing from the publisher.

To order additional copies of this book, contact:

Parson's Porch Books
1-423-475-7308
www.parsonsporch.com

Parson's Porch Books is an imprint of Parson's Porch & Company (PP&C) in Cleveland, Tennessee. PP&C is an innovative non-profit organization which raises money by publishing books of noted authors, representing all genres. All donations from contributors and profits from publishing are shared with the poor.

Life Lessons from the School Bus

Pre-Trip

What to Expect

This book is divided into three main sections. These sections are patterned after what a typical certified driver sees every day and is required by law to complete. Fortunately for you, the reader, there will be no fines assessed by the Department of Transportation of your state if you fail to complete them.

1. **The Pre-Trip** – The Pre-trip is what a certified driver must complete before he/she ever takes a commercial vehicle out on the road. It consists of many things, such as checking the lights, brakes, air pressure, adjusting mirrors, etc. For you, the Pre-Trip section is the place where you can become familiar with the layout of the book, what to expect from the stops on the route, and make sure you have everything you need to complete the trip.

2. **Route Stops** – Many commercial drivers, such as bus drivers, have to follow route sheets. These sheets provide the professional with a list of stops that need to be completed before the job is done. You will need to stop and read each story in order to understand each Life Lesson.

3. **Post-Trip** – The Post-trip is what a commercial drive does/fills out at the end of his/her day. During this time one is expected to re-inspect the vehicle, make sure everything is still in working order, and make positively sure (in the case of school bus drivers) that no sleeping children are left on board. Your Post-Trip will be a little different, but with one similarity: *never* let children sleep on this book.

Introduction

This is what you do: put somebody in a 40 ft-long, 33,000 lb steel box for several hours a day. Then, add your choice of a few dozen kids hyped up on candy after a party, a few drunken sorority girls, crying toddlers, fog, darkness, and swarming ants attracted to a forbidden pop-tart. Do this and what you will have either a recipe for disaster, or an average day on a school bus (except for the drunken sorority girls – that was *not normal!*).

Now, to the best of my recollection, I've met only one adult who said, "I always wanted to be a school bus driver." Most, like me, wound up taking the job out of desperation, because our spouses told us to, or because we were attracted to the crazy hours and summers off without pay. I'm convinced only a select few wake up one morning and exclaim, "*Hey!* I want to drive a bus! It'll be *fun!*" No, in my opinion, a sovereign God sets in motion a variety of calamitous circumstances to place drivers behind the wheels of school buses in order to teach us about life. The rest become transportation managers and dispatchers.

Therefore, after nearly fifteen years behind the wheel, I've compiled a collection of *mostly*-true anecdotes, a few serious observations, and a wealth of wisdom you'd be hard-pressed to find anywhere else, unless you've driven a school bus. However, don't feel you have to drive a bus, or even have a driver's license, to enjoy this book. Even if you've been banned from the road, the following stories will give you a license to laugh.

At the end of each story (names have been changed to protect the innocent – *especially* me) you will find two things, each meant to make you do an "emergency stop" (that's bus lingo) in your brain. First, there will be something called a "Life Lesson." This is the part where I, the brilliant author, will attempt to sound as wise as Solomon by relating a bus-driving story to everyday life. The "Life Lesson" will attempt to bring everything together in a flash of profundity, a moment in time when you will sit back and say, "*Wow!*" You may even shed a tear.

The second thing you will find is something I have decided to call "Route Suggestions." This is the part where I will leave you with some simple bullet-pointed suggestions designed to make your own *bus route of life* easier. Without them, you could run into dead end streets, make illegal stops, or find yourself out of fuel in the middle of nowhere with crying children wanting mommy and no way to radio for help. For heaven's sake, don't take these route suggestions lightly!

By the time you finish this little book, my prayer is that you will have done at least two of the following:

1. Made plenty of notes.
2. Laughed and cried at least ten times.
3. Bought more copies to give to others – because this one is now too special for you to loan or give away.
4. Been encouraged in one way or another.
5. Developed a closer relationship with the Giver of Life.

Come and ride with me! As we traverse the flat, wide-open tobacco fields of Kentucky, to the foggy-mountain curves and narrow city streets of Tennessee, something is bound to stick to your window.

Check List of Items Needed to Read This Book.

- Pencil or Pen: for making notes; preferably the quill of a goose.

- Highlighter: for doing what highlighters do.

- Ruler or Straight Edge: for making straight lines when you underline an important, life-changing point – like the ones you highlight with your highlighter.

- Flashlight: for reading in the dark – like when the power goes out in a storm, or when your spouse wants to go to sleep.

- Ear Plugs: to keep you from being distracted by things less important than reading this book.

- Credit Card: to purchase additional gift copies of this book – like for your worthless in-law, people who think bus drivers have it easy, and people who need a dose of truth.

- Sense of Humor: hopefully, you've figured that out by now.

- Open Heart: you never know when God will speak.

"Crank It Up!"

It may be a no-brainer to most of you, but you have to put the key in the ignition and crank a bus before it can go anywhere. You knew that, right? Well, believe it or not, there are a lot of journeys never embarked upon because the vehicles of life were never started.

At the beginning of each year a bus driver is given a list of "stops," which are the addresses where he will stop to pick up children to be transported. As you read through the pages to follow, you will be making twenty stops. Each one will be a different story that concludes with a lesson for life and a few pointers for down the road. But if you never get past this page the lessons will never be learned.

That's the way it is with life. There is so much to be learned, but learning only happens when we put the key in the ignition, crank the engine, release the brake, and move forward. You have to start somewhere to get somewhere. Otherwise, you're perfectly good bus is going to waste away in the parking lot as the tires rot and go flat.

If you learn nothing else from this book, learn this: *you were created for a purpose, and that purpose is to grow, to go, and to teach others what you know.*

Do you know where you are headed in this life? Do you wake up each morning with purpose and a plan to reach your goals? If not, why not? Determine right now that there is more to life than lazily waiting for something to happen. The greatest adventures can only happen when you decide to start the motor.

You've got the key, so crank up your engine, let your foot off the brake, and let's take this puppy for a ride!

Route Stops

1. Making a Way	13
2. Puke Breeds Puke	16
3. Losing Her Marbles	18
4. Which Way Do I Go?	20
5. No More Goodbyes	23
6. Tennis Balls	25
7. Are They Blind?	28
8. Say It with Boldness	30
9. It's Not Just About the Journey	34
10. Till the Storm Passes Over	37
11. Stormy Weather	40
12. A Small Observation	42
13. Hiding In Plain Sight	45
14. Maybe I Could Be a Poet	47
15. The Worst Field Trip Guide	50
16. Out of the Mouths of Babes	53
17. The Only Way Across	56
18. Try the Spirits	58
19. The Untamed Tongue	61
20. Unexpected Truth	64

Stop #1
"Making a Way"

Have you ever tried to merge into traffic, only to find that everyone else is in a bigger hurry than you? Try convincing a bunch of motorists on their way home that your school bus needs to jump into the flow.

Trying to Merge

Every time people see my kid transporter attempting to enter traffic from a side street, they say to themselves, "*Oh no! I can't get stuck behind a bus!*" It's like they go into panic mode, or

something. Don't they understand that it's not my intention to bring their world to a halt?

Without any compassion for me and my nerves, they pretend they don't see me. Honestly, drivers will look straight ahead like a horse with blinders on, knowing if they ever make eye contact they'd feel guilty, and drive past like I'm not even there.

Of course, there are the others who have more important places to be. Maybe they took a little too long on their morning jog, or maybe the secretary can't figure out how to make copies. Maybe little Junior, the class pet, must be first to put an apple on the teacher's desk...I don't know. They just hold up a hand, wave slightly, and give me a look that says, "*Sorry, but my schedule is too hectic to let you in front of me.*"

Making a Way

Here's a simple fact of life – not all publicity is good publicity, no matter what your Hollywood agent tells you. Believe me, no one wants to be known as the careless driver who hit a bus load of children and have his/her picture broadcast in HD during the evening news. That kind of publicity is bad for one's image.

At times a bus driver must be proactive. By knowing how people think, and with a little assertiveness, I can use my 33,000 lbs of diesel-powered yellow intimidation to create an opening in traffic. When necessary, by taking advantage of my vehicle's size, I can squeeze into traffic and make a way where there was no way.

Life Lesson
God can make a way, when there seems to be no way.

Referring to the time when the children of Israel were facing utter destruction at the hand of Pharaoh, the Psalmist said, "He divided the sea, and caused them to pass through; and he made the waters to stand as a heap" (Psalm 78:13). When God chooses to do something, nothing in heaven or on earth can stop Him. No decree of man, or law of nature, is an obstacle to the LORD of creation.

Do you think there is no hope, no way out? Do you feel like your options have run out? Trust in Jesus – He can make a way where there seems to be no way. God's a might big God, and He knows how to make a road through any obstacle you may face.

Route Suggestions

- When obstacles stand in your way, don't give up so easily; be assertive and show some initiative.
- Read *Matthew 6:25-34*. What does it say about worrying?

• Read *2 Samuel 24:14*. Someone once said, "When you come to the end of your rope, tie a knot and hang on." You might find it less stressful to simply "let go and let God." He will open the doors that need to be opened, make a way where there needs to be a way, and still hold you firmly in the protection of His mighty hand.

Stop #2
"Puke Breeds Puke"

It's the last thing a bus driver wants to deal with, but *puke* happens.

The Sorority Chick
In the introduction to this book I mentioned something about "sorority girls." Let me tell you what happened.

On a couple of different occasions I have been hired by a local university to drive a bunch of sorority girls and their dates to special parties. These parties are always themed, held in a previously-undisclosed location, and always involve adult beverages (for those 21 and older). Because no one is supposed to know where they are going, and because of potential alcohol consumption, all the university students attending must ride a bus.

One night I pulled into the parking lot where all the sorority girls and their dates were waiting to load. The only problem was that one young woman was already "loaded." In other words, cowgirl Jane (that's how she was dressed) had already wrangled up and downed a few beers. Somehow she got past the screening process only to stumble into my nightmare.

A few minutes after arriving, everyone I was to transport was ready to go, so off we headed to the location where the party was being held – on Lookout Mountain. But here's the thing: the roads up the mountain are curvy, and *drunken sorority cowgirls don't like curvy*. Honestly, it took only two curves before the sorority chick vomited all over the window and wall where she was sitting. Do you have any idea how hard it is to clean regurgitated Budweiser from between bus seats and the wall?

But it could have been worse. (*I would have included an illustration, but I've been too traumatized.*)

The Perfect Storm
Recently a driver in our area suffered a puking "perfect storm." One child on his bus got sick and orally relieved himself, which started a chain reaction. I'll never forget the driver's words over the two-way radio, "It's *everywhere*...all over...the bus is covered."

You see, there is an irrefutable law on school buses: *puke runs downhill* (or down aisles). So, when one kid started throwing up, six or seven others followed his example, leaving the bus to be washed out with a water hose. I never found out whether or not the driver threw up. I probably would have.

Life Lesson
Watch your mouth – and what you spew out of it.
The way you talk will influence others. Bad attitudes breed more bad attitudes, and what you end up with is a nasty mess.

Route Suggestions

- Don't drink and drive! Well, unless it's coffee – coffee *saves* lives.
- Never transport drunks up curvy mountain roads in your clean vehicle.
- Read the third chapter of the book of James (especially verses 3 thru 8).
- Think before you speak, and then speak wisely. Some messes are hard to clean up.

Stop #3
"Losing Her Marbles"

Once there was a little girl on my bus who cried over everything, especially when she didn't get her way. She ended up losing her marbles.

Snotty Susie
One morning this little girl – let's just call her "Snotty Susie" – was crying about how everybody hated her. Seriously, not two minutes after getting on the bus she started in with her *caterwauling* (the howling or wailing noise a cat makes). For the next 15 minutes the rest of the kids tried to console

her, but all she kept saying through the sniffing, slobbering and crying was "*Nobody* wants to be my friend! Everybody *hates* me! WAAAAAH!"

Fortunately, we reached the elementary school before everyone went deaf from the crying. Then, just as "Snotty Suzie" was stepping off the bus, a little boy who had gotten off in front of her looked back and said, "Nobody *hates* you, "Susie"; we just don't *like* you."

At least the little guy was honest.

The Great Giveaway
Well, that afternoon, when the elementary kids were getting on the bus to go home, "Susie" got on first and sat on the front row. "*Would you like a marble, Mr. Baker?*" she asked. "*No,*" I said, "*I have plenty.*"

"*What kind do you have?*" she asked. "*The round kind,*" I replied.

Then, as the other children entered the bus, just as soon as they walked past her, she would ask, "*Would you like a marble? You can have it for keeps. EVERYONE! Get your FREE marble, if you WANT one!"*

I asked, *"What are you doing? Why are you giving away your marbles?"* She said, *"Because I am going to MAKE them like me."*

Honestly, I felt sorry for the poor little girl. No one had ever taught her how to make friends.

Life Lesson
When we treat people poorly, and then try to buy their friendship with shiny trinkets, we end up losing our marbles.

"Snotty Susie" usually had a bad attitude about everything. She regularly talked mean to other kids, made fun of them, and then cried out in pain when someone wasn't nice to her. No one wanted to be her friend because she was NOT friendly! She couldn't even buy friends for a day.

Route Suggestions

- Don't try to buy your friends. If you do, you'll just go broke (marble deficient) trying to keep them.
- Don't let anyone buy YOUR friendship. Be a *real* friend to somebody who's a marble short.
- Read *Proverbs 18:24*. King Solomon said, "A man that has friends must show himself friendly." Short on friends? How can you be nice to someone today?

Stop #4
"Which Way Do I Go?"

Every school bus driver is a hero, but substitute bus drivers ("sub drivers") are in a class by themselves. I should know....I *was* one.

Sub Drivers Rule!
Unlike a driver that has a regular route, a "sub" is a driver that drives different routes every day. Whenever a driver gets sick, has to go to his grandmother's funeral, or gets fired for doing something stupid, a substitute driver is asked to cover that route. Most of the time, the call comes without any warning...or sunlight.

However, one of the problems that a substitute driver faces is figuring out where to go. Imagine being put in a vehicle with 70 children just out of class, wanting to go home. Imagine you are in a part of town you've never been in before. Imagine that you have no instructions or directions, but must depend on the kids (Heaven help us) to get you where you need to go. Been there...done that...*literally* got the t-shirt.

Now, try to imagine that the very ones that are trying to tell you where to turn don't *EVEN* know their rights from their lefts! It happened to me.....surely it did!

"I'm NOT Stupid"
I will never forget pulling up to an intersection and being forced to decide which way to go. I ask, "*Which way?*" The response comes back, "*Go right.*" So, that's what I proceeded to do, when, I swear, the conversation went something like this:

Kid 1: NOOO! Go RIGHT! You're going the wrong way!

Me: Wait, you said "Go right," so that what I was doing.

Kid 1: No you weren't...you're going left...I said "go right."

Me: I DID go right!

Kid 1: No, you went left.

Kid 2: You *did* tell the bus driver to go *right*, man, and that's what he did.

Kid 1: No he didn't! He went left!

Kid 2: Dude, you must not know your right from your left.

Kid 1: *Shut up!* Yes I DO!!

Me: (To Kid 1) Ok, let's get this straight. Which is right, and which is left? Hold up your *right* hand.

Kid 1: (Holds up his left hand)

Me: Hold up your *left* hand.

Kid 1: (Holds up his right) See, I *told* you. I'm NOT stupid!

Life Lesson
There is a right way, and there is a wrong way.

The right way may be the left way; but if the facts are not right, somebody's gonna get left. I know I'm right on this one. As a matter of fact, there is a verse in the Bible that seems to talk about the same thing. Proverbs 14:12 (NIV) says, "There is a way that seems right to a man, but in the end it leads to death."

How many times have you been on a road going the wrong direction? What did it take to turn you around? The thing about going down the wrong road of life is that we may never see the end of the road coming.

Route Suggestions
- Make sure of the direction you are going.
- Don't be afraid to admit you're lost (your wife already knows it).
- Make sure your source of determining right and wrong (or right and left) is reliable. You don't want to go the wrong way for an eternity, do you?
- Read *Proverbs 16:25*. What is that verse talking about?

Stop #5
"No More Goodbyes"

Some routines are more important than others. Everybody has them, even kids. What can we learn from them?

My Routines
I have my morning routines. Every morning I wake up between 5 and 5:30 am. If I don't forcibly poke the "snooze" button on my iPhone alarm several times, I have enough time to wake up, say a prayer, listen to a verse of Scripture (there's an app for that), and scroll through Facebook comments. If I sleep in too long, all I have time to do is brush my teeth, throw my clothes on, and go downstairs for a cup of instant coffee. After that is when I pre-trip my bus.

Everybody has their morning routines, even children. They even have a getting-on-the-bus routine which led me to think about life, living, dying, and meeting again.

Their Routine
Elementary kids will tell their parents "goodbye" before they board the bus, then they will do it again once they find a seat. Almost without fail my first and second-graders  will take ten seconds to hug and say "goodbye" at the stop, but then rush to lower the windows as we pull away in order wave and scream, "*Bye! Bye, Momma! Bye!*"

Later in the day, when I take these same children home, they talk and play with each other (sometimes too much) until they get close to their stop. They're usually not thinking too much about getting off the bus, but the moment they feel the bus slow down they gather their things and move to the door. As soon as the door opens they see their mom, dad, or granny...then scream...then run to their side...then embrace ... like it's been forever.

Life Lesson
Last "goodbyes" are never enough.

Even when we expect a loved one to pass away from a long-term illness, the moment of death is like that moment on the bus when a child leaves: the time for departure has been expected, but that last "good-bye" is never enough.

But *hallelujah*! Praise God for homecomings!!
I don't know about you, but I'm looking out the window. Yes, I'm enjoying the time I have with my friends and family down here, but home is just around the bend. Any moment the bus will be slowing down.

Route Suggestions
- Enjoy the ride, but don't let it drive you crazy; life is too precious to let others ruin it.
- Make sure you've got everything ready to exit the bus.
- Read *John 14:1-6*. Make sure you're on the right bus!

Believe me, once I get to my stop, I'll be jumping off and running to the House. I'll see family...I'll scream with joy...I'll run...then embrace...

Stop #6
"Tennis Balls"

Back when I first trained to drive a school bus, all drivers were required to complete an obstacle course. I don't know what they do these days, but one obstacle that I had to overcome is worth remembering – the tennis ball row.

Crazy Obstacles
The obstacle course was tough enough, but one test that we had to go through seemed totally off the wall. It was the last test, the last trial, the last obstacle of the day. All one had to do was drive a school bus across a parking lot, but without touching any tennis balls. What's the catch?

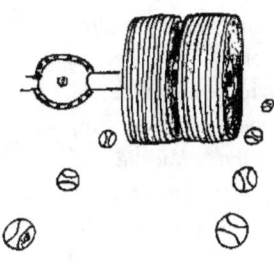

The right side of the bus, front tire and rear tires, was to go between two rows of tennis balls, the spacing of which only left 2 inches of clearance. In other words, you only had at most 2 inches on either side of the widest part of the back tires. Touch a tennis ball and you have to start over. Go over the tennis balls – you fail.

Really, I could see how this exercise taught precision driving skills, but what was the point. When on earth was I supposed to encounter a bunch of yellow balls on the highway? Little did I know a day would come when I would see first-hand the purpose for this lesson.

The Real Test
A few months into my driving career, I was asked to fill in on a route in the county. The route I was put on took me way out into farm country...tobacco country. After picking up a

few kids, my directions led me down a gravel road, way out amidst acres of Kentucky no-man's land. It wasn't too long until I came upon a creek. The only way to get across the creek was to drive my 15 ton bus over a homemade, log and plank bridge.

"*You have GOT to be kidding me!*" was the first words out of my mouth.

"No, this is the way we always go," said the boy noticing the terror in my face.

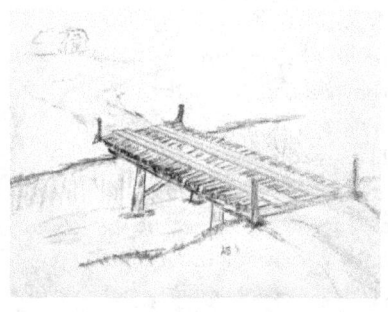

Trembling in my driver's seat, my muscles hardly willing to obey my brain's idiotic commands, I slowly began my crossing. Middle of the way through, as the bus was slightly rocking back and forth; I could see that my tires were barely on the wooden planks that lay across the logs. Then it hit me – "*That's why they had us drive through those tennis balls!*"

The next thought that came into my mind was, "If they had told me what they were training me for, *I would have found another job.*"

Life Lesson
Sometimes we are called by God to go through tests and trials which we don't understand. What we need to realize is that God knows what is ahead of us, what bridges we may have to cross. The reason for the lesson may not be obvious until the need for application.

Because you know that the testing of your faith produces perseverance, why not let perseverance finish its work so that you may be mature and complete, not lacking anything? – James 1:3-4 (*paraphrased*)

Route Suggestions
- Treat every trial in life like an obstacle course; you never know when you'll need the training.
- Take your training seriously; you may be the one responsible for carrying someone over to the other side.
- Ask your neighbors with rickety old bridges to invest in some concrete!

Stop #7
"Are They Blind?"

If there is one thing that makes me angry enough to spit nails, pound a steering wheel, clinch my teeth, and silently whisper vulgarities under my breath, it is: **People who run school bus stop signs!**

Running Stop Signs

I can't tell you how many times it has happened to me. In one morning I counted at least four times people blatantly broke the law (at least in our state) and blew right past me when my stop sign was out and flashing.

Honestly, I would like to know what goes through the minds of these idiots. What causes them to act so carelessly? Should they even be behind the wheel of a vehicle? Are they just careless, or are they blind?

One time, believe it or not, a motorist (older white male) came around from behind me on the side of the service door, the door where the students step out! He literally came within a few feet of hitting three middle schoolers!

What do you think I did? Well, what I *wanted* to do was chase him down with the bus and pin his car to a guardrail until the police arrived. What I *actually* did was call him an unflattering name that suggested his parents were not married at the time of his unfortunate birth. That was all I could do – he got away before I could get his license plate number.

A Friendly Warning
If you are one of those who think it's OK to run a school bus stop sign, especially if you have an important date, or just can't stand the thought of being held up another minute – *Somebody* is watching. Understand that every time you skirt the law, run the stop sign, and go your merry way – when I *can't* get your license plate number – *God* has got your number, bub!

Stop and think a moment. Every time you flagrantly drive through a bus stop, you put children at risk. You make your priorities more important than the lives of little children. Do you think that for one moment Heaven is on your side of the argument? Do you think that risking running over one of "these little ones" is any different than "despising" them? Do you believe in God? Keep running those stop signs and you will learn the lesson of the day...

Life Lesson
You will eventually reap what you sow (what goes around, comes around).
In his letter to the Galatians, the Apostle Paul warned: "Be not deceived; God is not mocked: for whatsoever a man soweth, that shall he also reap" (Galatians 6:7). The same can be said about those who run bus stop signs. One day you're going to get what is coming to you, *especially if you hit one of those children.*

Route Suggestions
- Pay attention and keep your eyes on the road; you never know when or where an unexpected stop sign may appear.
- Don't live in such a rush that a simple pause in your schedule will make you want to take unnecessary or unlawful risks.
- Thank God for the occasional "stop signs" in life; they're there for everyone's protection. Why run them and live with the regret?

Stop #8
"Say it with Boldness"

There comes a time when even a little kid may decide he's had enough. Essentially, that is what happened not long ago on my bus, and even a few thousand years ago on the plains of Judah.

The "Beyblade" Story
You see, for some reason, a few older elementary children kept aggravating a little kindergarten student named, let's just say, "Bill." Every time Bill would get on the bus, the first words he heard were, "*Hey, you got your Beyblades?*" Every day, every morning, it was the same question: "*You got your Beyblades?*"

    Note: *Beyblades* are little spinning top-like toys that, when set spinning and placed inside a plastic "stadium," will spin and bounce around until one knocks the others out of play.

    After a while, it started getting on my nerves. It wasn't so much the constant asking, but the constant trashing of the English language. It was never "*do you have,*" or "*have you got?*" No, it was always "*you got?*" Poor little Bill never made a sound. He would just walk quietly to his seat.

    Finally, about the time I was about to say, "*Will you illiterate examples of prenatal abuse put a sock in it,*" little Bill made his unexpected stand.

The Stand
Early one morning, shortly after a beautiful sunrise, I drove up to Bill's house, turned on my warning lights, engaged my brakes, and opened my service door, causing red lights to flash. Barely more than 3 feet tall, Bill had to grab hold of the rail as he struggled to make the climb up the staircase, each step a third his size. But with each step you could hear the young scholars, those brilliant wordsmiths, those

elementary-aged Einsteins, call out from their seats, "*You got those Beyblades? You got those Beyblades?*"

When his ascension to the top of the stairs was complete, he stopped and stood defiantly in the front of the bus, feet shoulder-width apart, fists clinched and placed on his waist. Without any warning, in the loudest voice a post-toddler could muster, he demanded..."SHUT THE F*** UP!"

"*WHOA!! Hold on there, little buddy! Dude, what did you just say?!*" I said, "*Son, you need to sit down...you can't say stuff like that...I will talk with you in a few minutes.*"

I had never heard, nor seen a little child with so much bravado. Like biblical David facing a bus load of mentally-challenged Goliaths, Bill decided he had heard enough. With the confidence that his words would be heard; with the confidence that just the right combination of words would demand respect, he stood on his soap box and demanded attention, never showing a hint of fear or intimidation. Without question he made his point. The other kids were shocked and silenced. Sadly, however, somebody taught him to talk that way.

Life Lesson
When you take a stand for what you believe, don't act cowardly or intimidated. Be strong in your convictions and speak with boldness. Being meek and mild has nothing to do with being milk toast. Cowards do not deserve respect, or an audience.

Even though little Bill chose to use inappropriate language, his indignation, expressed with boldness, earned him my respect. I couldn't help but admire him. After becoming weary of taunting words (on and off the bus), he felt it was time to make a stand.

Little Bill's stand was a little like the one "little David," the shepherd boy, made before the 9 foot-tall Goliath. Essentially, David told the giant to "*shut up!*"

> *David asked, "Who is this uncircumcised Philistine, that he should defy the armies of the living God?"*
>
> *Then David said to the Philistine, "You come to me with a sword, with a spear, and with a javelin. But I come to you in the name of the LORD of hosts, the God of the armies of Israel, whom you have defied. This day the LORD will deliver you into my hand, and I will strike you and take your head from you. And this day I will give the carcasses of the camp of the Philistines to the birds of the air and the wild beasts of the earth, that all the earth may know that there is a God in Israel. Then all this assembly shall know that the LORD does not save with sword and spear; for the battle is the LORD's, and He will give you into our hands."*
> *– 1 Samuel 17:26b, 45-47 NKJV*

When a person dares to speak with boldness, the "Goliaths" may laugh at first. But on the other hand, a defiant stand against the cowardly bullies of this world may shut their mouths.

May we all learn a lesson from little Bill's outburst. No matter your size or your age, your education or your status, there's a time to stand for what is right; don't be afraid to be heard.

Route Suggestions
- When the time comes to make a stand, do it like you mean it!
- When Truth is on your side, don't be ashamed or afraid – be BOLD!
- Avoid ticking off quiet kindergarteners.

Stop #9
"It's Not Just About the Journey"

Some people say "it's all about the journey." *Really?* Tell that to a parent after you deliver her child to a different house.

Going Places
When I am driving a school bus, I am always trying to watch my surroundings. There are always dangers on the road; everything from potholes, to crazy drivers. It is also important to watch my gauges. By watching things like my temperature, fuel, and air-pressure indicators I can tell if my bus is operating correctly. The last thing I want to do is wreck, but neither do I want to run out of fuel or break down with a bus load of kids.

But the thing that I have to know, if nothing else, to make my job a success, is where the heck I'm going.

Now, I am not talking about simple directions. The "*rights and lefts*" are the supposedly simple directions that tell a driver where a kid lives and how to get there. However, knowing where the children live and picking them up is only part of the job. **Getting them to the right school is the ultimate goal.**

What's Important
That's the part that's most important, you know. You can pick up all the kids in town, but you need to get them to the right destination. The safest driver in the world would still be harming the young skulls full of mush if the last stop he made was at the mall, the wrong school, a playground, or the city dump. The last stop *has* to be the school the kids

attend. Otherwise, the whole trip was in vain. If I don't get the kids to where they are supposed to go, I haven't done my job. My journey has ended in failure.

Life Lesson
It's not so much about the journey, but more about where the journey ends.

Miley Cyrus sang a song in one of her movies that said, "It ain't about how fast I get there. It ain't about what's waiting on the other side...*it's the climb.*" The problem with that logic is this: what if you're climbing the wrong mountain? All that hiking up the side of the rocks may earn you a few bragging rights, but what's the point if you're not getting anywhere, or worse, you're going the wrong way? (Read Proverbs 14:12)

Speaking of his own journey, Paul the Apostle said, "I have fought the good fight, I have finished the race, I have kept the faith. Now there is in store for me the crown of righteousness, which the Lord, the righteous Judge, will award to me on that day and not only to me, but also to all who have longed for his appearing" (2 Timothy 4:7-8 NIV).

For Paul, there was something to look forward to at the end of his race. He realized that there was a reason for the "fight" and a purpose for "keeping the faith." He saw at the end of his journey a reward that made the hard travel, the bumpy and bruising roads, and the "climbing" worth it all.

Roads lead to places. A journey, by definition, needs to have a destination, or you're just walking in circles. Sadly, many on the road of life are content with the journey, never caring that the "rights and lefts" they are following are flawed. The final stop leaves them without joy, without purpose, without hope, empty, and without God.

Route Suggestions
- Don't take the kids to the wrong school.
- If you're going to go climbing, make sure how tall the mountain is; you may need some oxygen equipment.
- Don't take directions from Miley Cyrus; she has a foam pointer, but she doesn't know how to use it.
- Grab yourself a copy of the world's best-selling road map for life – the Bible.

Stop #10
"Till the Storm Passes Over"

One day a strong storm front moved through our community. I was in the bus. *NOT* a good idea.

The Storm

Normally, the middle and high schools for which I drive dismiss at 2:15. On one particular day, because of a coming storm, school dismissal was delayed until 2:30. That was a smart move. It would have been really dangerous to be on the road with a bunch of children and a tornado coming. So, instead of staying on a bus, the other bus drivers and I went inside the school to wait things out.

It's a funny thing, those storms. Even after the warnings were given, even though we knew a storm was close by, outside the sky above the school was blue with hardly a cloud. What we could not see was a fast-moving front coming our way and hidden just out of our view, just behind a nearby mountain.

Because I knew that rain and high winds were on the way, I decided to quickly step outside of the school and onto my bus to put up the windows. That was at 2:15......at 2:17 it was still calm......at 2:18 the storm hit like a freight train.

The following is what I posted on Facebook from my iPhone:

- 2:18 pm "Storm is on us at lookout valley. In bus. Not good. Think was a bad idea."
- 2:21 pm "Lying on floor."
- 2:21 pm "Just a little scared."
- 2:23 pm "Hail."

- 2:24 pm "Hope somebody is praying."
- 2:30 pm "Whew! Bad stuff is over. Kids will be getting on bus soon. They held them in the school until the storm passed. Was scary."

The reason I got down in the floor, as opposed to sitting in my seat, was because I was afraid that broken glass might start flying around. I also thought that I might be safer on the floor if a tree came looking for my head. Who knows? All I know is that while I was on the floor – while the bus rocked and the wind roared – I prayed.

I didn't get off the bus because the wind was so intense, and opening the door would have been difficult, if not impossible. Not to mention, I had no idea if I would have been blown away or hit by a head-seeking oak branch. At least in the bus there was some metal protecting me. But on the other hand, it would have been a *lot* safer in the building. The bus was a *bad* idea.

The Result

As a result of the storm, there were hundreds of calls to the police for help. Trees were down everywhere blocking roads, taking down power lines, and even crushing cars and damaging houses. As a matter of fact, I had to wait for nearly an hour for a power line to be cleared, just so my bus to get down a little back road. It was a mess.

Ironically, just a week or so after this storm hit, tornadoes plowed through Georgia, Alabama, and Tennessee, including my community. Had it not been for this storm we might have been caught off guard. We heeded the warnings, and I was *not* on a bus (But I was looking out of a window in our church as the remnant of a tornado spun through the parking lot – not smart).

Life Lesson

Sometimes storms come when you *least* expect them, even when you expect they will come. When they do, it is best to find shelter in a place that can weather the storm.

> *"The LORD is my rock, and my fortress, and my deliverer; my God, my strength, in whom I will trust; my buckler, and the horn of my salvation, and my high tower (Psalms 18:2)."*

When the storms of life hit, the best place to be is within our Savior's protective hand. The flimsy philosophies of this world are no better than a school bus in gale force winds. Till the storm passes over, resting safe within His arms is the best place to be.

Route Suggestions
- Never seek shelter from strong winds or tornadoes in a vehicle, no matter the size.
- Look up the song "Till the Storm Passes By" by Dottie Rambo.
- Take weather warnings seriously and never take unnecessary risks.
- IF caught in a storm like I mentioned, stay off Facebook and pray! What could you expect your stalking friends to do, anyway?

Stop #11
"Stormy Weather"

One person's ordinary weather is another person's storm of the century. If you don't believe me, just ask a school bus driver – or ANY driver, for that matter – in the South.

The Ice Age
Not long ago, Tennessee was getting frosted on a near-weekly basis. As a matter of fact, the persistent whiteness was beginning to annoy me, almost as much as Joel Osteen's smile. Our schools had to close; parents had to take off work to stay with their children; convenience stores sold out of toilet paper,
bread, and milk; and civilization as we know it ground to a halt. Yet, as we were panicking over nothing more than the *threat* of snow, schools up north were trucking through blizzards and turning snowmen into hood ornaments.

Southerners don't spend a lot of money on snow removal equipment; it's just not that necessary during a normal winter. So, when it *does* snow only the main roads get serviced, if at all. The mountainous and rural back roads, where most kids live, are rarely salted or plowed. Typically, people 'round here just wait a day or so for the arctic terror to melt. Until then, driving is dangerous, so buses stay parked and empty.

Ice Truckers
My wife was in Chicago visiting family when a full-fledged blizzard hit. She sent me a picture of a school bus transporting children in weather that would have given a Tennessee school administrator heart failure. There must

have been ten inches of snow on the road! We are likely to call off school when frost covers a windshield, but evidently Yankees (is that politically correct?) drive their kids to school on a snow plow!

What's the difference? Why do some people drive in the snow while others freak out? People up north are used to the snow; Southerners are not. To people in Chicago our worst weather was just another work day.

Of course, it does make me wonder, though. What do those "snowbirds" think of our heat, humidity, and lung-clogging pollen? Tennessee's a wonderful place to be in August...like when it's 108 and every mosquito knows your address.

Life Lesson
What you may think is no big deal could be earth-shattering to someone else. The key is to never view another person's problem as insignificant.

Show grace and mercy to those who aren't handling things so well; yours may be the strength and encouragement they need to make it through. Who knows, a time may come when you need help out of an unexpected blizzard.

Route Suggestions
- Learn to tell the difference between northern dry fluff and southern wet terror. All snows are not alike.
- Always be prepared for bad weather by carrying with you a blanket, a flashlight, a kerosene heater, dry wood for a fire, a battery-powered two-way radio, a satellite phone, and someone willing to walk five miles for help.
- Take it easy on people who find it hard to endure the potholes you consider normal. For those who have been used to a smooth road, the average pothole can really shake them up.

Stop #12
"A Small Observation"

I drive kids around all day. You could call them little, but they can tell when someone is a little different. Sometimes they say things, too.

Politically Incorrect
Once you read what this Life Lesson is all about, you may think I'm being politically incorrect, insensitive, or mean-spirited. You may think that the title is inappropriate and beneath me (OK, that was bad). You may even tell me that I should not make fun of those who are "vertically challenged."

But if you *do* think I am making fun of short, small, or otherwise non-tall people, then think again. I am only being humorous at their expense to make a point. Actually, it won't be at their expense for long; I am going to pay the bill.

Children can be Cruel
You know it's true. I know it more than I want to. When driving around with a bus load of elementary children, one hears a lot of cruel comments coming from their angelic, crumb-crunching mouths.

Little girls, as well as little boys, can get downright mean with the things they say. However, they consider their words purely harmless. The concept of lasting consequences is beyond their comprehension. They have yet to sit through months, or years, of $150 per-hour counseling.

Because kids can be cruel, intentionally or not, I try to steer them (literally) away from the opportunity. But on one occasion, even though I did the best I could, the kids jumped at the chance to gawk and laugh. I will never forget what I saw.

Choosing Not to Hear
Not long ago I was driving my school bus down a two-lane road when just ahead of me I spotted a dwarf...a short guy...a midget...walking by the curb. Immediately, I knew what was about to happen.

Right ahead of where this guy was walking was a place I had to make a stop. Sadly, I could not just speed on by, but had to slow down. When the first child saw this little man it didn't take long for the 20+ others to shift over to that side of the bus to take a look. In an instant there was laughter.

But in all honesty, the laughter was not all that loud. My kids are aware that stuff like that makes me angry, so they try not to get caught. So, only if one had been really listening or paying attention could that person have heard the giggles and jokes. The little man on the road didn't want to take any chances.

As soon as I started to pass by this 3ft-tall little bald guy with biker tattoos (wearing a tank top and little jeans), he did something that really broke my heart – *he put his finger in his ear*. He knew what was coming, and maybe he didn't want to hear because...

- He had heard cruel laughter before
- He expected to hear it again
- He knew what kinds of things would be said
- He did not have the will, nor the ability to defend himself
- He decided not to listen, but to close his ears

Sadly, many are convinced what other people say about them is true. The jeers and the laughter not only offend, but cut deeply, causing irreparable scarring and pain.

How many have given up? How many have quit defending themselves?

One of the characteristics of a true Christian should be that he defends the defenseless, the ones who cannot speak up for themselves. Psalm 82:3 says that we should "defend the poor and fatherless: do justice to the afflicted and needy." Couldn't this also apply to standing up for those who are made fun of or mocked?

Life Lesson
The next time you are around someone, even a child, who makes fun of another person, stop and take the time to "defend" and "do justice."

The next time *you* are tempted, consider what you are doing.

Route Suggestions
- Keep your fingers out of your ears when you drive.
- Always treat others with respect, even those who look different.
- Consider the words of Jesus: "Thou shalt love thy neighbor as thyself" (Mark 12:31). Would you want to be laughed at because of something *you* couldn't help?

Stop #13
"Hiding in Plain Sight"

One lesson nearly cost me dearly. It had to do with missing what was hiding in plain sight.

The Story
As you can see in the picture, a typical school bus has two mirrors immediately to the left of the driver window (besides the convex mirror below). With mirrors everywhere, driving is made much safer and easier, even in heavy traffic. What you don't see is what is on the other side of the mirrors.

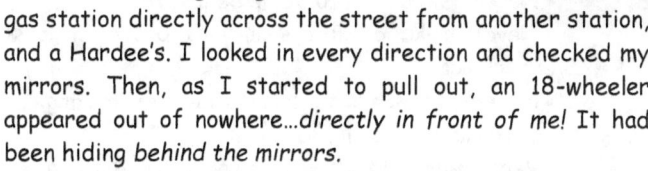

(This picture was taken at the very spot an accident could have taken place.)

I was beginning to exit a gas station directly across the street from another station, and a Hardee's. I looked in every direction and checked my mirrors. Then, as I started to pull out, an 18-wheeler appeared out of nowhere...*directly in front of me!* It had been hiding *behind the mirrors*.

Take a look at the picture. Right behind the top mirror sat a Peterbilt. I never saw it. What saved me was taking my time and being cautious. Had I rushed on forward I may have pulled right into the path of that big truck. Only going slow and expecting the unexpected made the difference.

Life Lesson
So many tragedies in life could be avoided if only we would take the time to "consider our ways."

> "Now therefore thus saith the LORD of hosts; Consider your ways" (Haggai 1:5).

Do we stop to think about where we are going? Do we take the time to make sure there is nothing hidden behind the obvious? Sometimes our judgment can be clouded by the determination to move forward with our plans. Wisdom understands that the Enemy loves to capitalize on things hidden.

For example, how many people have fallen into financial ruin because they rushed into a business deal or bought something too expensive? Many times there are dangers lurking in the fine print or hidden in words we don't take time to understand. Even though the path may look clear, it never hurts to take one more look before proceeding. Ironically, big dangers can hide behind the very things meant to point them out.

Route Suggestions
- Never get too comfortable behind the wheel.
- Never make quick assumptions based on past experiences.
- Never let someone rush you into making an uninformed decision.
- Read *Psalm 119:105*. How important is it to have a light when driving down a dark and unfamiliar road? Where does this verse say we can find light for the road of life?

Stop #14
"Maybe I Could Be a Poet"

There are times when bus drivers have to sit and wait between routes for children to get out of school. Some read. Some hang out with other drivers. Some sleep. Others write bad poetry.

An Impromptu Poem

    I'm sitting at the school
    Waiting for some children
    To get done with their recess
    Then to my bus to get in
    My coffee's disappointing
    I'm not awake enough
    To see the brighter side of things
    Man, this job is rough
    At least I have a job
    At least I have some income
    I've got a place to live
    Food enough, and then some
    But screaming, crying, slapping
    "Life's over" comments flying
    From eight-year-olds who rule the world
    Make me think less of the driving
    And more seriously of cliff diving

I wrote this in one sitting, so pardon me if it's not of Shakespearean quality.

Life Lesson
Don't quit your day job to follow a dream if you ate pizza the night before. Just sayin'.

I have written several songs, a few of which have been recorded. I have also written some decent poems along the way. But it would take a whole lot more talent than what I've got to make enough money to feed my dog, much less my family.

Some people think it's totally cool to walk away from a regular paycheck at a regular job in order to pursue a lifelong dream, like being a movie star. Unfortunately, many dreamers overrate themselves and only find out too late that they're not as good as they thought.

Wait! Does this mean you should never try? Should you never take any risks or step out in faith? Of course not! Just don't be too impulsive. Proverbs 21:5 in the New Living Translation says, *"Good planning and hard work lead to prosperity, but hasty shortcuts lead to poverty."* The key to following a dream is to have a plan.

Route Suggestions
- If you have a dream to do something or be something (like go to the moon or be a movie star), find out what it would take to see your dream come to reality. Ask questions. Do your research. Talk to people who are where you want to be.
- Talk with people who don't know you, people who will give you an honest appraisal of your talent. They won't try to discourage you (normally), but they'll usually be able to tell if you've got what it takes.
- Once you determine if your dream is realistic, get to work. Like others have wisely said, every journey begins with a first step. Make a plan, get your stuff together, and go for it.
- Understand that you may get discouraged if you try to rush your dream; good things take time.

However, the journey to where you're going could bring you as much joy as the realization of your dream.

Stop #15
"The Worst Field Trip Guide"

One day I transported 80 kindergarteners on a field trip to a mountain forest. Do you have *any* idea how loud 80 excited 5 year-olds can get when confined in a 40ft.-long steel box on wheels?

Teacher Talk
I couldn't help overhear the advice school teachers were giving to the little crumb crunchers on the bus, then later after they unloaded. One warned, "Don't pick anything up from the ground; you won't be able to keep it, anyway." Another said, "Don't bounce on the swinging bridge; just look over the side." *Seriously?* How can you tell a 5 year-old not to jump on a swinging bridge and then expect him *not* to jump on the swinging bridge?

SIDE NOTE: I remember when our oldest daughter, Alicia, who was around 12 or 13 at the time, went with me to visit the old capital building in Frankfort, Kentucky. In that old landmark is a genuine floating staircase on which Alicia decided to jump up and down. I asked, "What are you doing?" She calmly replied, "Trying to see if it will fall." I said, "Two things...First, it's been here since 1827 and hasn't fallen, yet you think your scrawny self is going to break it? Second, *why* would you want to be on it if you *could* make it fall?"

Anyway... the best piece of advice from the teachers was clear enough: "Do *NOT* get off the trail!" But again, honestly, how many kids actually listen to instructions that make sense? I mean, you take a child that's never been out of the suburbs to a forest with plants taller than their apartment buildings and you expect them not to run amuck? Therefore, I decided to speak up and add some clarification to the teachers' warning. I said, "Because if you get off the trail, we *might* have to send the *DOGS* after you."

Who knew one little girl was afraid of dogs? *I didn't!* ...Cry baby.

Bad Advice
So, that got me to thinking: what would be the *worst* advice to give 80 children before a trip into the woods?

"BAD ADVICE"

- Don't worry about your lunch box; the forest is *full* of pretty berries.
- As long as the animal is smaller than you, go ahead and pet it. It won't mind.
- Hey, bounce on the swinging bridge! It's just like a trampoline.
- Of course! Rules are *meant* to be broken.
- Bears? *What* bears? This is Tennessee, kid. We don't have bears. You're thinking of Chicago.
- I don't care *what* your mom said, poison oak is a hoax. Don't your parents have oak furniture? Does it make you itch? *See*, she *lied*.
- Who can get closest to the edge? Let's find out.
- Whatever you do, *don't* stay on the trail. Trails are for *babies*.
- Snakes are overrated, misunderstood jump ropes. They want you to play with them.

Life Lesson
Thankfully, when it comes to the wilderness of life, there is One who always gives good advice.

In his famous Psalm 23, David wrote, "*Yea, though I walk through the valley of the shadow of death, I will fear no evil: for thou art with me; thy rod and thy staff they comfort me."* God urges us to stay on the path that He has already walked, which is why Jesus said in Matthew 4:19, "Follow me."

He knows the difference between *good* fruit and the *forbidden* kind.

Route Suggestions
- Don't give vague instructions to children; they need specifics.
- Go check out the old capital building in Frankfort, Kentucky – but don't jump on the staircase.
- Never get to the point where you are too proud to listen to instructions or advice. For example, you may have been down this road before, but your tour guide has been down it more recently. There may have been some changes of which you are unaware, like a washed out bridge or recently released bears. Oh my!
- Read *Psalm 23*. Was David walking alone? How could this Psalm relate to your life?

Stop #16
"Out of the Mouths of Babes"

Why is it that so many place such a high premium on what children say? Why should we "listen to the children?" Sure, every once in while they say something cute or insightful, but on a regular basis? Get real! They may be short, but each one is *not* a little Yoda.

Buy Your Own House

One morning a self-proclaimed genius decided to share his "wisdom" with me. According to this young man, a fifth grader, it was better to *not* buy a house together, or share your money, with your wife (if you get married). Why? *"Because your wife may end up becoming a prostitute and kick you out and make you pay alimony."* Excuse me?

How I wanted to pray for that poor boy! Where was he learning that stuff? Is this what he thinks of *all* women? Is this what he thinks of marriage? What kind of future do we have if kids like that keep growing up and taking over? He is definitely NOT a child I want to listen to.

If Children Ruled the World

But there are those who swear that true wisdom can be found in the words of young children. Forget the need for a lifetime of experience, listen to the wisdom of those who just learned to wear pull-ups and cut their own meat. If we did what the bleeding hearts wanted us to do - *listen to the children* – where would we be right now?

No one would ever work ... *except those who need to work so that others would not have to work.*

Every day would be Christmas, Halloween, and summer vacation ... *as long as someone else buys the gifts, provides the candy, and drives them to the beach.*

There would be peace on earth and no more wars ... *except when someone disrespects you or takes your candy.*

Everything should be available for the asking whenever it is wanted ... *as long as we don't have to be the ones providing it for someone else.*

There would be no need for multiple television channels ...*only Disney, Nickelodeon, MTV, and VH1.*

Everyone would have everything they always wanted, whether they needed it, or not ... *and still act like brats that never get anything they want.*

No one would ever eat at home, only restaurants ... *then complain about their weight.*

Education, if desired, would be determined by what the child thought was important ... *like college courses entitled "The Sociology of Miley Cyrus: Race, Class, Gender, and Media (Skidmore College)."*

Teachers, Doctors, Policemen, School Teachers, and Ministers would be disrespected and maligned ... *while movie stars, rap and rock stars, and vulgar athletes would be deified.*

Animals would be considered equal with humans ... *except when it came to leather clothing and Happy Meals.*

Hate would be outlawed ... *unless someone disagreed with you.*

Church would be nothing but fun and games - *none of that judgmental, right/wrong stuff* - with cookies for all to enjoy.

Now that I think about it, maybe the children are in charge already!

Life Lesson
Be the adult you want your children to become.

King Solomon begged, "Listen, my sons, to a father's instruction; pay attention and gain understanding" (Proverbs 4:1 NIV). Unfortunately, so many parents themselves act like spoiled children. They live lives that teach kids to get all they can get, even if they have to take it by force. They use and abuse their spouses, cheat on each other, then wonder why their kids talk to bus drivers about prostitutes and alimony.

Route Suggestions
- Don't give children everything they ask for – that's not love; it's enablement.
- Ask your children tough questions about life, questions that might clue you in to what they may do as adults: Why by faithful? Why not steal? Why not lie? You might be shocked, even terrified.
- Read a chapter a day from the book of Proverbs (31 chapters, one for every day of the month). Read them, and then read them with your kids.

Stop #17
"The Only Way Across"

Sometimes we have to take a leap of faith, or at least drive on a bridge by faith.

My Fear

I am not afraid of many things. I am not afraid of the dark. Monsters don't keep me awake at night. Even spiders and snakes don't creep me out too much, as long as I am prepared for their presence.  However, there is one fear that besets me – the fear of bridges – *gephyrophobia*.

Despite my fear of falling great distances to a painful death amidst crumpled steel and shattered concrete, my job requires me to drive a large school bus across an 80 year-old death trap 4 times a day.

The picture you see was taken from inside my bus at the very point where the bridge is the highest and possibly weakest (and most likely to kill me). But because I need extra money to take care of my family, and because I want to keep my job, the route I drive requires me to put my faith in this bridge.

There is no other option.

The Only Bridge

Similarly, when the Apostle Peter was faced with the choice to either follow Jesus or turn away, he realized there was no other Bridge to eternity. When hundreds of others doubted the Messiah and left, Peter stayed. He said to Jesus, *"Lord, to whom shall we go? Thou hast the words of eternal life"* (John 6:68). Even when Peter didn't fully understand what Christ was doing, he still believed.

> *Neither is there salvation in any other: for there is none other name under heaven given among men, whereby we must be saved.* – Acts 4:12

Life Lesson
Sometimes we exhibit faith, whether we like it or not.

Sometimes we have to trust, even when it's not easy, even when it seems a little crazy. But when life is hard; when nothing seems to make sense; what option do we have except to trust God? Jesus is the Bridge that has never failed. He is the Bridge that spans the ravine between man and a Holy God (1Timothy 2:5). Even though it may involve trust like you've never known, the *only way across is Christ*. Have no fear.

Route Suggestions
- Avoid old, dilapidated bridges if at all possible.
- Press down on the accelerator as you drive over a bridge; if you're going fast enough when it collapses, you might make it to the other side, anyway.
- Don't be afraid of faith; you exhibit it all the time – like when you sit in a chair, crank your car, put your money in a bank, or flip on a light switch. Do you *really know* the chair will hold you up, or that the car will crank? No, you just have faith that they will.
- Do you want to know God and please Him? Do like Peter and step out of the boat (Matthew 14:28). Understand this: without faith, it is *impossible* to please God (Hebrews 11:6).

Stop #18
"Try the Spirits"

For the record, this stop has nothing to do with ghosts or alcohol. However, I might have been taking some pretty strong cough medicine when I wrote it.

"Stripped"

Bob "Apple" Smith, a bus driver for the county, has a lot to explain. A quick look at his bus will let you know why. It is stripped. Stripped of EVERY-THING!

According to Bob, shortly after dropping off the last of his children, he made a quick "personal" stop. It was during his "personal" stop, which took longer than he anticipated (probably due to the excessive amount of jalapeños Bob insisted to be put on his eggs for breakfast), that vandals supposedly stripped his 88-passenger Thomas Built bus.

"Once I was finally able to finish my business," Bob said, "I went back outside and said, '*I'll be dang!*'" He went on to say, "Those little hoodlums worked quicker than piranhas on a pig!"

The Link

No wonder! Bob had parked his bus in one the most notorious places in town. For months the police have been answering calls from stranded motorist who could do nothing more than cry after doing their "personal" business. Fortunately, an unbelievable link may have been found.

After investigators did some research, Bob was not the only one who had eaten eggs at a particular diner on Downtown Street. It seems that more than one patron of

"Slick Sam's" had eaten eggs before having to stop just blocks away to make an emergency "deposit." Coincidentally, those same patrons had their automobiles stripped.

The only problem for Mr. Smith is the additional time it would have taken to strip the large bus. Some are questioning whether or not there may be seeds of deceit at his "Apple" core. It was not long ago another driver, Margaret "Snoopy" Jones, overheard Bob say, "I am tired of this job, but I'm not going to quit without getting a medal." Ms. Jones insists he was speaking code, meaning "metal" when he said "medal." This is still under investigation, but questionable, however. It seems that Ms. Jones has a record of saying, "Bob was always the 'bad Apple' in the bus driver barrel."

Life Lesson
For heaven's sake, don't believe everything you read.

Sometimes things like this can be seen as funny (I hope), but many are sadly deceived in issues that have eternal significance. The Bereans did not even take the Apostle Paul's words at face value. They "tried" his words by comparing them to Scripture (Acts 17:10-11). You see, no buses got stripped by vandals, and you could easily prove this by doing a little research. As matter of fact, the bus in the picture *was* stripped, but only for spare parts (it had an engine fire that made it too expensive to fix). But so many people will take anyone's word, believe any hearsay, hold to any old rumor or fable, rather than take the "noble" route of the Bereans and "search the Scripture."

Wise Solomon said that "simple man believes anything... (Proverbs 14:15a)." Therefore, "believe not every spirit, but try the spirits whether they are of God: because many false prophets are gone out into the world (1 John 4:1)." Gullible people fall for anything.

Route Suggestions

- Ask several questions to help determine whether or not a story is true. *First*, is the story consistent, or do certain things not add up? *Second*, does the story help make sense of reality (i.e., does it adequately explain what you see?)? *Third*, are the supposed facts verifiable?

- Before you believe a story, make sure you verify the source. For example, not everything you read on the internet is true. Yes, I know that's hard to believe.

- Always try to tell the truth; it will make you more believable. You never know when you'll need to tell a story that's almost too crazy to believe.

- The next time you're approached by a guy that smells of alcohol and urine, yet is asking for money to repair the fan belt on his broken down car – all so he can get back home to Montana to feed his ailing great aunt – how will you be able to determine if he is telling the truth? *Hint:* look back at the first point.

Stop #19
"The Untamed Tongue"

First there was smoke. Then there was cursing. Then, after a few warnings, the cuffs came out. For some reason one girl couldn't keep her mouth shut.

Help Appreciated
To begin with, I'm the only decrepit old person on my bus. However, if I were to drive a bus that transported handicapped students, then I would be required to have another grown-up ride along with me, like an assistant or bus monitor. But like most other drivers, I have to transport "regular ed" students by myself.

For the most part, being the only adult on a bus full of students is not that difficult, especially if the students being transported are easy to get along with. It's when there are a lot of younger children (as many as 80) or unruly teenagers on board that make having a second set of eyes truly a blessing, if not a necessity.

On one occasion in Kentucky I *did* have an adult monitor, and it was she who noticed the smell of smoke...which led to some interesting drama.

Where there's Smoke
We were probably only ten minutes into our route when my bus monitor smelled marijuana. *"Stop the bus! Stop the bus!"* she yelled from behind my head, nearly scaring me to death. After I made an emergency stop and secured the parking brake, I asked what was going on. The older, heavier, and much-meaner-than-me African-American lady replied, "They're back there smokin' pot! Can't you smell dat?"

For the record, no, I had no idea what burning marijuana smelled like. I was brought up in a Baptist preacher's home, went to Christian schools, and didn't even go to my first movie in a theater until I was ten years-old!

Where was I supposed to become acquainted with weed? And, what's more, how was I supposed to know that high school kids tried to disguise the smell of pot by inserting the drug inside Black & Mild cigars? Who knew?

Anyway, with the bus now pulled over, I requested my dispatch send out a police car. In the meantime it quickly became obvious to my worldly-wise assistant that the hash had been thrown out of the window and was in no one's possession. Yet, when the police got there they still went to the back of the bus to question students and search bags. Everyone was very polite and compliant, that is, except for one smart-alecky teenager sitting up front.

She Wouldn't Shut Up

Let's be very clear, the kids in the back of the bus being questioned were black; the girl up front was white. This matters because the girl up front starting accusing the police of racism as she protested their work. She said things like, "You only be doin' this 'cause they *black*...this is r*acist*! You ain't got *no* right to arrest them! They *innocent!*" One of the policemen said, "Young lady, this has nothing to do with you, so just be quiet." Unfortunately, the young protester's tongue kept flapping.

For several minutes, while one policeman calmly searched and questioned the respectful pot-smokers in the back, the second policeman continued to warn the foul-mouthed teen up front to shut her mouth. "They did nuthin' wrong! Leave them the f*** alone! You're gonna have to f******* arrest *me*, you *pigs*! They *innocent!!!*" she'd scream.

Then, after giving her one more opportunity to be quiet, the white girl cursed the policeman one more time. In a flash the 80-lb. trash-talker was jerked out of her seat, marched down the steps, and then out onto the grass beside the bus. I couldn't hear any more of the conversation, but there was a lot of finger-pointing from the cop and squared shoulders from the girl. Eventually, the officer took all he could take, turned her around, put her in cuffs and escorted her by the elbow to a waiting squad car.

Life Lesson
When it's time to speak, speak. When it's not, shut the heck up!

I wonder how many times the poor girl had back-talked her parents and her teachers. Had she ever been taught to keep her mouth shut when it was none of her business?

"Led captive by her tongue"

The book of Proverbs is full of verses warning the foolish to tame his tongue. One verse says that whoever controls his mouth and tongue keeps his soul from trouble (21:23). Another warns that whoever "openeth wide his lips shall have destruction" (13:3).

Ultimately, the wisdom of Proverbs 6:2 became reality for Miss Potty Mouth: "Thou art *snared* with the words of thy mouth; thou art *taken* with the words of thy mouth." Cuffed and hauled away – sounds about right.

Route Suggestions
• There are times to speak up, and there are times to be quiet? How can you tell the difference?
• Compare the following verses: Proverbs 17:28, Proverbs 31:8, Ephesians 4:29, and James 3:2-10. What did you learn from these?
• Think about the way you talk, because language is a mirror to the soul. What are your words reflecting about you?

Stop #20
"Unexpected Truth"

Every once in a while a bus driver, or anyone for that matter, may find himself saying, "I didn't see *that* one coming!" In other words, every once in a while something happens; somebody says something that you would have never imagined. Let me tell you about one of those "once in a while's."

Spitting Accusations
Kids are always doing stuff to each other to be aggravating. You have probably witnessed children throwing spit wads, taking items out of another's book bag, or hiding a child's shoe right before her stop. No? Well what about spitting on each other?

Oh, yes, children are well-accustomed to spitting on each other, especially boys. Now, they never admit to doing it; they usually blame it on the one kid with no salivary glands. But there was this one time when a boy on my bus accused a girl of spitting on him when she actually didn't. How do I know that she didn't? She showed me proof!

So, "Jack" hollered from the back of the bus, "Mr. Baker! 'Jill' spit on me!" Before I could rationally respond, another voice came from the back, the voice of the accused, crying, "No I didn't – he's lying!" Since I was in the process of driving and there was no place to pull over and deal with the situation, all I could do at the moment was respond with a simple request: "STOP SPITTING!"

A moment passed, then Jill came up to the seat behind me (which is dangerous and against the rules, by the way). "Mr. Baker," she said in a tone laced with disgust, "I did not spit on Jack; he spit on himself after he spit on the seat."

"*What?*" I asked. "He's spitting on the seat?! That's *gross*!" Incidentally, this is one of those times when I find it appropriate to ask: why do people of any age find enjoyment in recreational spitting? Why waste perfectly good saliva when there's nothing necessarily nasty to expel from one's mouth?

Anyway, a moment or two later, Jack came up to share his side of the story. "Mr. Baker, Jill *did* spit on me! See my shirt? See, this is her spit...she spit on me! See?"

I couldn't argue with what I saw. There, as plain as the marks on a Dalmatian, were wet spots where something *liquidy* had collided with his shirt. *Somebody* had spit on him.

"Jill!" I yelled, "Why did you spit on Jack?" From the back of the bus came an insistent reply, "But I *didn't*! He spit on himself just to get *me* in trouble!"

The Truth Comes Out

Where's Solomon when you need him? Why can't school buses be equipped with portable DNA equipment? How was I supposed to determine who spit on who? How could I prove who needed to be punished with a stern warning and a verbal reprimand? The answer came in a way I never would have dreamed, but I will never forget.

"Mr. Baker..." Jill had made her way back up to the seat behind me, again while I was driving. "Jill, you need to sit down!" I told her.

"But Mr. Baker..." Let me just pause here to try to describe Jill's way of saying my name. Jill spoke with a slightly non-emotional, matter-of-fact, drawn-out southern drawl. It sounded more like "*Miiis-turr Buh-ayyy-kurr...*"

"Mr. Baker, I didn't spit on Jack; he spit on the seats and then on himself to make it look like I did it," she said. "But I *didn't*, and I can *prove* it."

"Really," I asked.

"Yes sir," Jill replied. "You see, Jack was eating green candy, and the spit on his shirt was green – mine is not...*SEE!*"

At that point, just around my right shoulder, came the arm of a little girl. Attached to that arm was a palm, and in that palm was half an ounce of spit – yes, *spit*! It looked like a blob of clear silicone!

"It wasn't *me* that spit, 'cause *my* spit is clear, seeeee Mr. Baker?"

I couldn't argue with her. She proved her point. There was the proof puddled in the palm of her hand, clear as day. I nearly threw up.

Life Lesson
We may not like it, but sometimes the truth is hard to stomach – and nothing like what we expected.

The simple fact is that truth isn't always pleasant; more often it is nasty. No woman wants to hear the truth when she asks, "Does this dress make me look fat?" No man wants to hear the truth when he asks, "How did I do with the laundry?" But sometimes the truth has to be told to make a difference. Unfortunately, to play off the words of Jack Nicholson in *A Few Good Men*, many can't handle the truth.

For example, there is a saying that goes, "You shall know the truth, and the truth shall make you free." Do you know where that saying came from? It came from Jesus. He said, "If you continue in my word, then you are my disciples indeed; and you shall know the truth, and the truth shall set you free" (John 8:31-32). The part that is hard for many to stomach is the part where He says, "If you continue in my word..." In other words, in order to know the truth that will set one free, one must be a follower of Jesus Christ.

Some say that truth is relative, that it changes with the circumstances of life. Others have said there is no truth, only perception (Gustave Flaubert). However, without truth there can be no lie, no wrong, and no remedy for the spit on some kid's shirt, not to mention the darkness in our hearts. But when we follow Jesus, we can rest assured there is Truth to know, for He said in John 14:6, "I am the WAY, the TRUTH, and the LIFE..."

Route Suggestions

- Don't ask someone to tell you the truth about how you look, how well you're doing your job, etc., unless you're willing to hear the truth.
- Don't "kill the messenger." If someone does try to tell the truth, don't get angry when they say the dress makes you look fat. Just get angry because they weren't sensitive enough to change the subject.
- When faced with a tough situation, one that demands you make a wise decision, ask God for help. James 1:5 says, "If any man lack wisdom, let him ask of God..."
- Read the book of John in the Bible. Make a list of the claims that Jesus made. Was He telling the truth? For the atheist or agnostic, that may be a truth too hard to handle, but it *will* set them free – if they believe.

Post-Trip

Recalling the Route

Before each morning run, everything about a school bus is to be gone over with a fine-toothed comb, much in the same way any other commercial vehicle is to be inspected. In a similar way, at the end of every day, the bus driver does what is called a "post-trip" inspection. This is the time to make sure everything is still in working order and that no children are still on the bus, possibly sleeping under a seat. However, before we kick the tires and check the lights, let's do a little reflecting.

It was a short route, wasn't it? Most bus drivers would love to have a route with only twenty stops, but yours was quick and easy, done in no time. As a matter of fact, it was over so quickly that it might be good to think about what you've read.

What was the most memorable moment?

_____

_____

_____

What was something you learned?

_____

_____

_____

Did you miss a stop? Can't remember? Then why not go back and read it again?

Child Check
One thing that school bus drivers must always do is check for sleeping children. It would be more than tragic to leave the bus while a child was still on board, alone and unattended; it would be criminal. Can you imagine how scary it would be to wake up from a long ride in a cold or hot, dark and lonely place? No parents...no friends...no idea how to get help...just terrified.

You've read about some of the children I've encountered. Some are in real need of adults who care. We don't always know what a child's home life is like, but we do know that children need positive adult role models and influences.

List a few of the positive adult influences in your life?

_____

_____

_____

How would your life have turned out differently if they had not been "on the bus?"

_____

_____

_____

One of the things that I have learned over the years is that I don't necessarily have to say anything to a child in order to be a positive influence. You see, I am prohibited by law from sharing my faith with the kids I drive around, but that doesn't mean I can't be an example of kindness, maturity, respect, and dependability. My actions can have long-term effects on young people, especially those who have few positive adult role models at home.

Your actions are always being observed. List a couple of things you could do differently or improve upon that may help a watching child become a better adult?

_____

_____

_____

System Check

Now that we are sure there are no children on the bus, let's make sure the bus is still in good condition. After all, morning comes pretty early, and the last thing you want is to encounter a problem (or miss it entirely) in the pre-dawn darkness. While there's still sunlight and time to get things fixed, let's go over some essentials.

☐ ***Any engine noises or warning lights?*** Believe it or not, a lot of people have gone to their graves ignoring the clear and unmistakable signs that something was wrong. How's your heart? Been to the doctor lately? When's the last time you had a real physical? Been feeling any strange pains? Our bodies were designed to warn us when something is breaking down.

Right now, write down anything that's not quite right about your body or how you feel. Don't ignore any warnings.

_____

_____

_____

Now, make a point to have these things checked out! Someone is counting on you!

☐ ***Check the brakes.*** I know it seems illogical to see if the brakes are working after it's obvious you've come to a complete stop, but work with me on this.

Driving a bus full of kids can be stressful, as can a lot of other jobs. But if you never take time to slow down and stop for a while, then one day, when you least expect it, you're going to run into a brick wall and hurt a lot more people than just yourself. Do you have any hobbies? What do you do to relax and have fun?

Jot down some things you'd like to do totally unrelated to your line of work.

_____

_____

_____

Don't let stress get the best of you. Learn how to slow down without crashing.

☐ ***Check the lights.*** There are a lot of lights on a school bus. But the most important lights on any vehicle are the headlights. Without headlights, when the weather is bad or when it's dark outside, how could you tell where to go? Blinkers are important. Warning lights and brake lights are important. But if you can't see where you are going, what good are all those other lights?

If there is one Truth from this book I'd like to get across, there is a Light for the road of life. A flashlight (or "torch," if you're in the UK) is good for the average path; high and low beams are good for the highway; but something more is needed to pierce the darkness of life's uncertain road.

> • Thy word is a lamp unto my feet, and a light unto my path. - *Psalm 119:105*
> • The statutes of the LORD are right, rejoicing the heart: the commandment of the LORD is pure, enlightening the eyes. - *Psalm 19:8*
> • For the commandment is a lamp; and the law is light; and reproofs of instruction are the way of life: - *Proverbs 6:23*
> • But all things that are reproved are made manifest by the light: for whatsoever doth make manifest is light. - *Ephesians 5:13*
> • For thou wilt light my candle: the LORD my God will enlighten my darkness. - *Psalm 18:28*

If you'd really like to see what's ahead of you, I'd advise turning on the light of the Bible. Unless, of course, you like stumbling around, running into ditches, etc.

Radio In and Check Out

I have the rare privilege of being able to keep my bus at home. I don't have to drive in to a bus garage, park my car, get on a bus, run my route, come back to the station, get in my car, and then go home. No, my bus stays right beside my house in the parking lot of the church I pastor.

However, because I am allowed to drive my school bus home, it is important that I use my two-way radio to check in with my dispatcher. It's important for them to know that everything is OK. If something is wrong, they need to know. If I'm doing well and on schedule, they need to know. Doing my part helps the dispatchers do their part.

This is what I'd like for you to do: radio in, email, send a smoke signal, message on Facebook, tweet, send a candy gram, or something! Just let me know how you are doing and what you think of this book. *I want to hear from you!*

Do you have comments or questions? Would you like to have me out to speak? Would you like to join the discussion about *Life Lessons from the School Bus*? Below is some helpful contact information.

- Email: **LifeLessons.SchoolBus@yahoo.com**
- Like our page on Facebook (Life Lessons from the School Bus)

For immediate spiritual help, call **1-888-NEED-HIM**

Dedication Page

Most of the time, the "dedication page" is found somewhere near the beginning of a book; however, this dedication page has been placed at the end, and for a good reason. Those to whom this book is being dedicated are used to coming last in line (and missing out on the best food). This book is dedicated to all those like myself... bi-vocational pastors and ministers.

Those who go into ministry, if they're doing it for the right reasons, do not do so in order to get rich. Despite what many people think, most pastors are not wealthy, do not live in big houses, or drive Jaguars. As a matter of fact, the majority of ministers have part-time jobs. Following in the tradition of those like the Apostle Paul, more and more ministers have to "make tents" in order to survive. Bi-vocational pastors and ministers work in the "secular" world, as well as the "sacred."

Because of the odd hours that allow for daytime hospital visits and other ministerial duties, many pastors find driving a school bus the perfect fit. But not all pastors can drive a bus; not all have the ability or temperament. Therefore, this book is dedicated not only to school bus drivers, but to all those who would wish to earn a full-time living from ministry, but can't. This book is dedicated to all the servants of God who serve His people with humility, compassion, and hard work in the church house, but also in the bus, out in the field, in the factory, on the roof, and a thousand other places. Not only do you live and work in the trenches where your congregants struggle through life, you do whatever it takes for the sake of the Gospel, and the people who need it.

You may not feel like it, but you are the real heroes. You are making a difference in the real world where real people live. You are part of a long, honored tradition, one worthy of much more respect than you normally receive.

God bless you!

www.ingramcontent.com/pod-product-compliance
Lightning Source LLC
Chambersburg PA
CBHW072105290426
44110CB00014B/1842